CORN-FED

poems by
JAMES STEVENSON
with illustrations by the author

GREENWILLOW BOOKS
An Imprint of HarperCollins*Publishers*

Corn-Fed: Poems
Copyright © 2002
by James Stevenson

All rights reserved.
Printed in Hong Kong by
South China Printing Co.
(1988) Ltd.
www.harperchildrens.com

Watercolor paints and a
black pen were used to
prepare the full-color art.

Library of Congress
Cataloging-in-Publication Data

Stevenson, James, (date)
Corn-fed / by James Stevenson.
    p.   cm.
"Greenwillow Books."
ISBN 0-06-000597-1 (trade).
ISBN 0-06-000598-X (lib. bdg.)
1. Children's poetry, American.
[1. American poetry.] I. Title.
PS3569.T4557 C65 2002
811'.54—dc21   2001033261

10 9 8 7 6 5 4 3 2 1
First Edition

For Chuck, with love

CONTENTS

Yesterday Larry sold
used cars.
Last night it snowed
and snowed.
Today he's selling hippos,
buffalo, and sheep.

I've been attacked by a rooster,

Kicked by a horse, chased by hornets,

And bitten by a seal.

Each time

I was surprised.

You never know

What's on somebody else's mind.

On my side of the table, it's ATO CHUP.

On your side, it's TOM KET.

But both are very good.

Want to take a picture

Of your chimney?

Want to get your cat

Out of a tree?

Want to get a little closer

To the moon?

Westside Rentals

Will be glad to help.

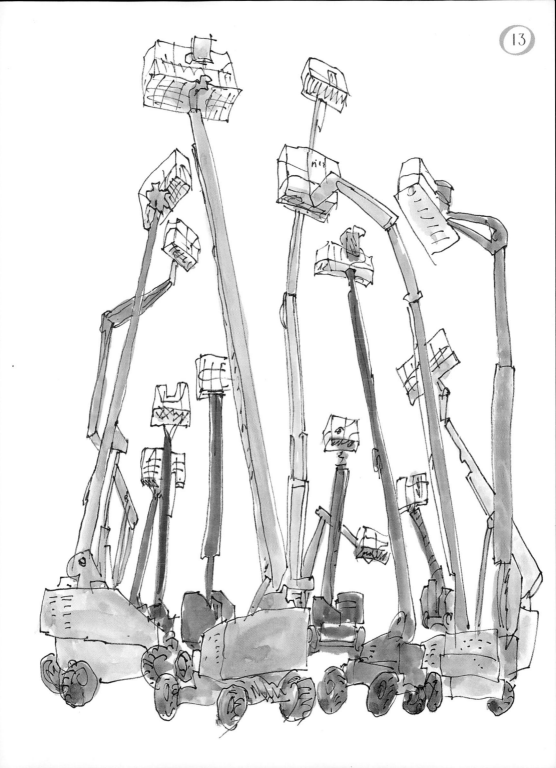

13

THE SIGN IN THE RESTAURANT WINDOW

MAKES YOU WONDER,

IS THIS A BOAST,

OR A WARNING?

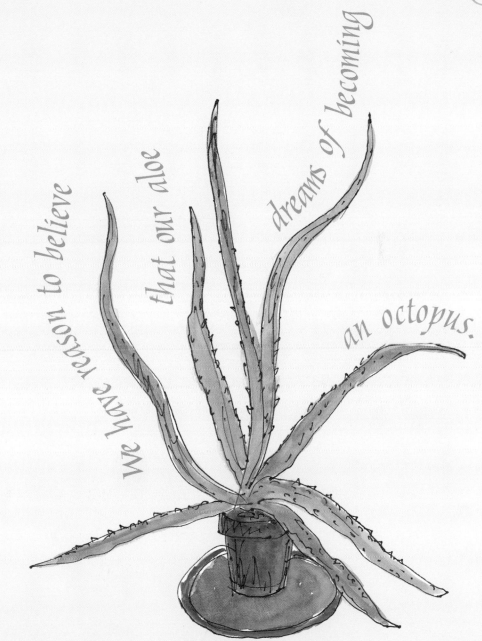

we have reason to believe that our aloe dreams of becoming an octopus.

Cold winds whip

Through their bones,

But summer will come,

And hot, noisy days

With many lives to guard.

If you take
3 tablespoons
of
mayonnaise,

1 cup
of
baking
powder,

3/4 cup
of
chunky
salsa,

1 pint
of
sour
cream,

1 teaspoon
of red
pepper,

2 teaspoons
of thyme,

3 tablespoons
of
mustard,

the juice of
4 lemons,

1 cup
of
olive
oil,

2 cups
of cocoa,

5 teaspoons
of
soy sauce,

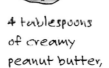

2 sweet
pickles
(chopped
fine),

4 tablespoons
of creamy
peanut butter,

2 cans of
lentil soup,
and
mix together, put in a large pot,
and let simmer for 2 hours,
it still won't taste
very good.

OVER THE YEARS

THE OLD GATE HAS DONE

A PRETTY GOOD JOB,

I GUESS. . . .

MOST OF THE ROCKS

ARE STILL THERE.

Somebody
brought
a red ball
to the park.

Some dogs stared at it.

Some
dogs
sniffed
it.

Some dogs dared it
to try and roll away.

Some dogs
guarded it.

Some dogs chased it.

Some dogs
wrestled over it.

Some dogs
grabbed it and
chewed it.

And some dogs
just didn't care
at all.

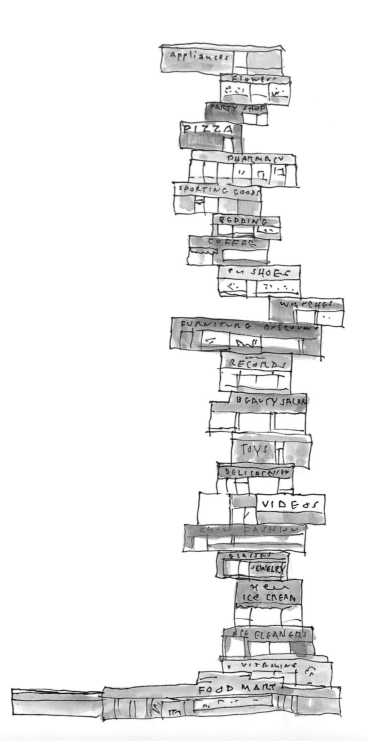

The Mall is

Such an ugly place.

Would it look better

If they

S
T
A
C
K
E
D

I
T

?

Not everything that runs

On the railroad tracks

Is a train.

But what these are,

You tell me.

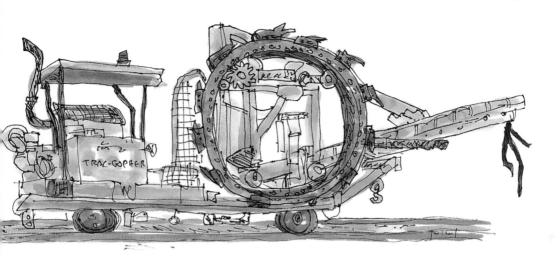

Compared to all

The skinny white yachts

In the marina,

This old tug is

One tough cookie.

The movie palace
Called the Shore
Closed years ago,
Says a man on the corner
With some time on his hands.
He says it was the best—
Double features all day long.
I'm wondering:
If you didn't like a movie,
Could you stand
On that fancy balcony and
Watch the Atlantic Ocean
Rolling in
And let some popcorn
Drift down seven stories
To the street?

FOR RENT

FOR RENT

Once a bike has discovered
What it's like
To run fast and free,
It just might try to escape.

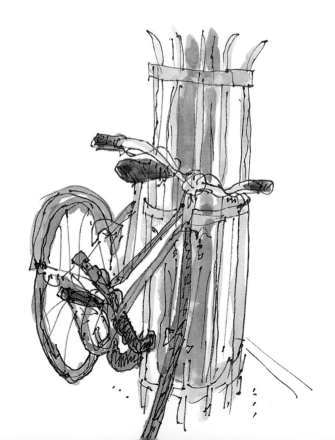

WHEN YOU WALK DOWN THE SIDEWALK,

MOST OF THE TIME YOU KNOW

WHAT THINGS ARE FOR,

BUT SOME OF THE TIME

YOU DON'T.

At the planetarium,
Small children stare
Out the windows
Of the buses,
Looking for the universe.

I love dawn,
Especially with
New York City
Under it.

When opossums get scared,

They pretend

To be dead.

But this one,

Lumbering across my path

At dawn,

Decided dying

Wouldn't work,

Since I had spotted him

In perfect health.

So he looked at me

With his two pink eyes,

And I looked at him

With my blues,

And we went

Our separate ways.

On the front of
The rusted mailbox,
You can make out
The words STORAGE BOX.
(But it doesn't say
For how long.)

Mt. Grunge

Mt. Everest

In the Himalayas

Is over 29,000 feet.

Mt. Grunge is only

A little over five,

But it is the highest peak

Of the Grimy Range,

Which runs along the side

Of Meadow Street,

At least until

The snow melts.

Want your shoes repaired?

Go to Mr. Girardi.

He's got everything he needs.

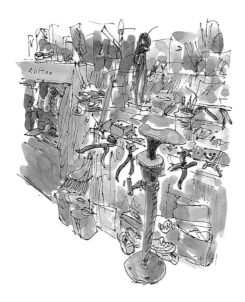

Mr. Girardi will get it done.
(He always does.)

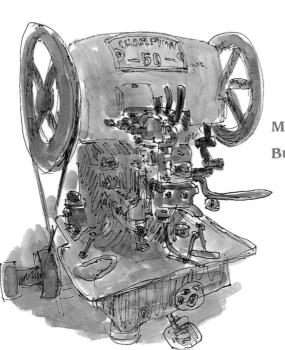

Maybe not tomorrow,
But soon.

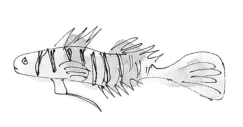

Did you ever wonder
Why fish look
So different,
While the rest of us
Look so much alike?

At the zoo,
Everybody looks at
The monkeys,
The birds,
The snakes,
The alligators,
The polar bears,
The penguins,

And the seals.

But nobody looks
At the pigeons.